The Domain of Rambouill[illegible]

Sophie Cueille, *researche[illegible]*

Rambouille[illegible] paradise for hunters. For several centuries its plentiful game attracted some of the most prestigious crowned heads in French history. Charles VI, François I, Louis XIV, Louis XV and Louis XVI all hunted in the forests around Rambouillet. Situated between the town and the park at the edge of this immense domain, the chateau reveals the exceptional refinement of its interiors only to the curious visitor. The elegance of the kingdom's finest 18th-century carved wooden panelling, the delicacy of the Empire decoration and the azure glow of the Delft room are set off by the opulence of the furniture, on loan from the state collections and in keeping with the chateau's role today as a presidential residence, one of the Republic's finest. The charm of the place resides too in its landscape and gardens, meticulously tended since the 17th century: the still waters of the majestic network of canals, the winding river, the vast meadows and forest avenues leading to unexpected garden buildings, masterpieces of picturesque or pastoral architecture.

A fortress at the edge of the Yvelines forest

Jean Bernier's chateau

In 1368 the knight Jean Bernier, councillor and master of petitions in the King's household, purchased from Girard de Tournebu a building described at the time as a 'manor-house and lodging'. In 1374, Bernier decided to transform this house into a fortified castle surrounded by moats. The ensemble occupied an irregular pentagonal space with a triangular main building flanked by turrets. A curtain wall enclosed the courtyard and joined up with a large tower and fortified gatehouse. To date, no documents have been found to give a clear idea of what the façades of this castle looked like; successive building campaigns have completely altered its primitive state. During this same period, King Charles V was building the fortresses of the Louvre and the Bastille. Bernier's works at Rambouillet may be seen then as a response to the royal order of 19 July 1367 which decreed that all the kingdom's chateaux should be fortified.

King Charles V in Paris, greeting the Emperor Charles IV in 1378. Miniature by Jean Fouquet, *Grandes Chroniques de France*, 15th century (Paris, BNF).

The country house of the Angennes family (1384-1699)

Ten years after its reconstruction, the castle was sold by Bernier's son, Guillaume, to Regnault d'Angennes, the King's 'premier esquire trenchant'.♦ For the next three centuries, the property was to remain in the Angennes family. A text of 1399 describes the chateau as 'a fortified mansion surrounded by moats of one *arpent* in surface [roughly an acre], with a covered bailey in front of this building, two stabling yards, a monumental portal, prison, garden, meadow, pond and mill.' The passages of English soldiers between 1425 and 1428 apparently caused some damage. Jean II d'Angennes and his wife had to undertake consider-

♦***Trenchant:*** *during the* Ancien Régime, *this high office was associated with the King's table. The 'premier esquire trenchant', was originally entrusted with carving the King's meat.*

The so-called François I tower, vestige of the first building erected during the 14th century.

able work on the building. In their will they declared that since their marriage in 1456, they had used all their resources for the 'repair, upkeep and embellishment' of their property. But we do not know exactly what this work entailed. Under Jacques d'Angennes (1514-1562), captain of the guards of François I, the estate was enlarged to encompass land in the territories of Auffargis, Poigny, the castellany of Essarts-le-Roi and various properties situated between the original estate and these new acquisitions. This good game country attracted François I who was a keen hunter. In March 1547, while staying at Rambouillet, the King died of a general infection, at the age of fifty-three. According to tradition, he expired in the upper chamber of the tower, giving this structure a royal cachet which probably helped to assure its conservation.

Jacques d'Angennes not only extended the grounds but also embellished the building. He commissioned a large room in the Italian style, with walls lined in marble by the master mason Olivier Ymbert. The main staircase, in brick and stone, was constructed at the same time. Ymbert, who came from the village of Saint-Léger-en-Yvelines, was also responsible for the construction of the chateau of Thoiry, between 1560 and 1564.

Portrait of François I by Jean Clouet, about 1535 (Paris, Musée du Louvre).

The Marquisate of Rambouillet

In 1612, under the reign of Louis XIII, as a reward for its services to the crown, the seigneury of Rambouillet was elevated to the rank of a marquisate. The Angennes family now figured amongst the most eminent in Paris society. Catherine de Vivonne, the wife of Charles d'Angennes, is remembered in French literary history as the Marquess of Rambouillet (1588-1665). Under the name of Arthénice, in the family's Paris town house, she held one of the most famous literary salons of its time. The guests were received in a place which has earned an enduring reputation, the 'Blue Chamber'. Here, members of cultivated society vied with each other in the composition of mannered rondeaux, conundrums and metamorphoses, all contributing to the enrichment of the French language. During their stays at Rambouillet, the guests would watch plays. In 1636, Jean Mairet's *Sophonisbe* was particularly appreciated, a play largely forgotten today. That summer, the poet Vincent Voiture wrote 'All the allurements, the graces, the passions / All the virtues which shine forth in our day / Have, for the last month, held court / At Rambouillet...' In other words, Rambouillet was the fashionable place to be. Julie d'Angennes, the daughter of Charles and Catherine, joined in at these gatherings. She is remem-

Portrait of Julie d'Angennes (Rambouillet, Town Hall). The young woman is holding a garland of flowers, an allusion to the collection of madrigals and sonnets that the Duke of Montausier offered her in 1642.

bered today for the collection of poems *La Guirlande de Julie,* which her future husband, the Duke of Montausier, dedicated to her. The estate, which came into his possession as Julie's dowry, was considerably enlarged, with new lands acquired between 1670 and 1681. Several biographers of Jean-Baptiste de La Quintinie, celebrated gardener of the King's kitchen garden at Versailles, mention that he also created an orchard at Rambouillet.

After the marriage of Julie's second daughter, the domain passed into the hands of the Duke d'Uzès. But, because of the deplorable state of the Uzès family fortunes and for lack of a direct heir, the chateau was then sold to one of this family's creditors, Fleuriau d'Armenonville. Several documents describe the property in 1699, shortly before the sale, as 'a large building situated at the end of a courtyard and on either side of this, two wings which are attached; at the end of one of them is a large tower surrounded by moats.' The chateau itself contains 'a chapel, several rooms with fireplaces, antechambers, wardrobes, lumber rooms, kitchen, pantry, cellars, the whole roofed in slate.' Mention is made of a 'bailey court coming up to the main building and enclosing a dovecote, stable, granary, carriage house with a gatekeeper's lodge, a grand portal with a pavilion over it, all these covered in tiles.' The grounds comprise 'a large park in which there are trees for timber, young plantations of oak trees and a tree nursery, a grand canal, a large lake, other canals, a pond, a large flower bed, meadows, arable land, pasture, several dwellings for a menagerie and for the keepers, an ice-house, a garden with fruit trees and espalier walls, separated from the park by wooden palisades, the whole estate surrounded by walls.'

La Guirlande de Julie
To the left: frontispiece of the work illustrated by the miniaturist Nicolas Robert in about 1642 (Paris, BNF).

To the right: *Zéphyr* by Nicolas Robert, about 1642 (Paris, BNF), illustrating the first sonnet entitled *Zéphire à Julie*, written by the Duke de Montausier, author of fifteen of the sixty-two poems which make up the collection.

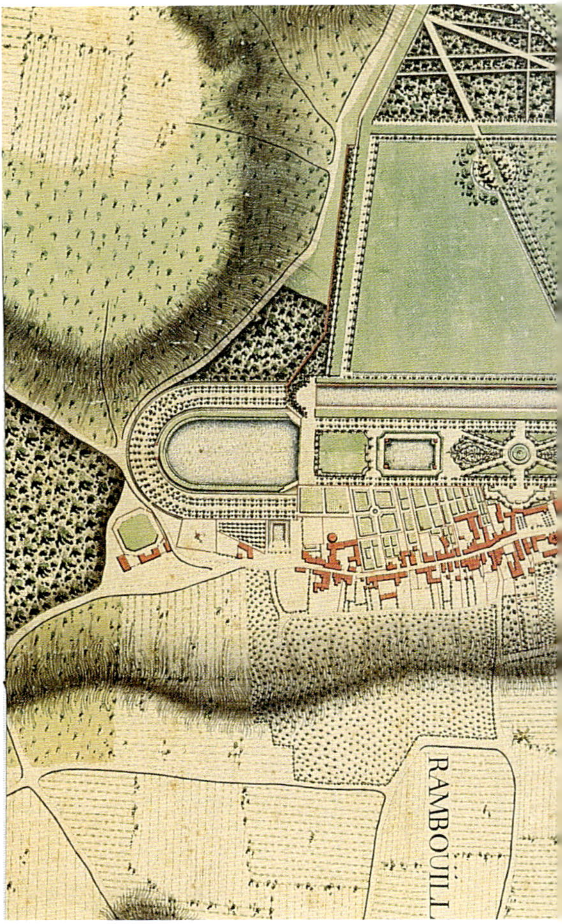

The art of perspectives

The composition of the garden for Fleuriau d'Armenonville

(1700-1705)

Joseph Jean-Baptiste Fleuriau d'Armenonville (1660-1728) was a financier who occupied positions as Intendant of Finances from 1690 to 1701, as general director of Finances and then as Lord Chancellor (*Garde des Sceaux*). He acquired the domain for the relatively modest sum of 140,000 *livres* and then, in the space of only five years, spent a further 500,000 on embellishing it. Although descriptions at the end of the

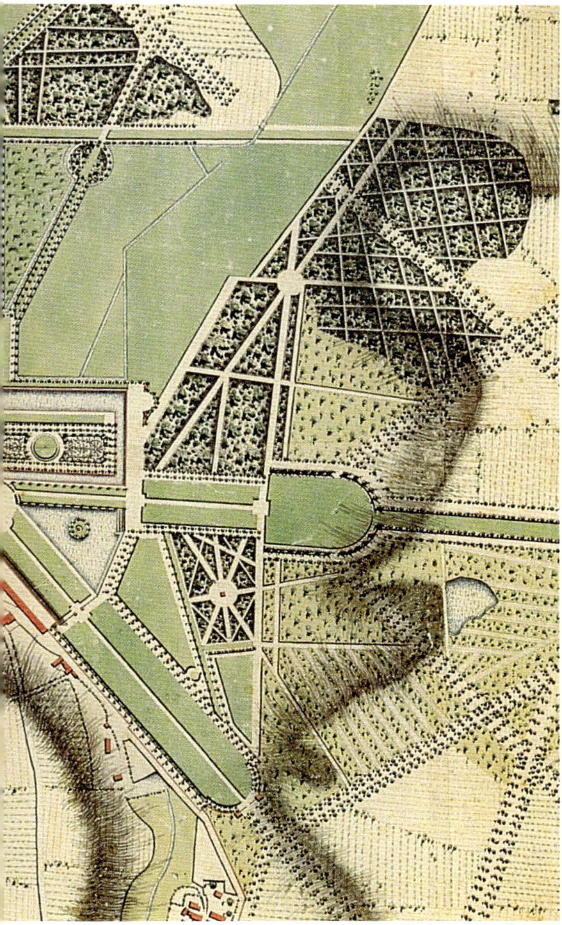

General plan of Rambouillet, dating from the first quarter of the 18th century, showing details of the water features in the park and the town below the chateau (Paris, Archives nationales).

previous century mention a canal, it is Fleuriau d'Armenonville, according to tradition, who was responsible for developing the gardens and giving the chateau a new setting in a formal, French-style park. A map drawn up in 1708 shows the park after this work. The visitor's eye is drawn along generous perspectives marked out by flower beds and water features, exploiting the natural resources of the marshy meadows. A broad canal was cut along the axis perpendicular to the southwest façade of the chateau, prolonged in the distance by a greensward. Another canal lines the flower beds directly in front of the chateau. To the left, after the box-edged beds, there is a succession of three small lakes of different forms. Sculptures by Simon Mazière, Pierre Legros and René Frémin adorn the park. In 1701, the marquisate is described as being located 'in one of the most fertile parts of the kingdom', possessing 'a beautiful park and country residence with several ornamental lakes, canals, ponds, terraces, flower beds, kitchen garden and orchard.'

The Count of Toulouse dressed as grand admiral of France, copy by Jean-Baptiste Charpentier, painter to the household of the Duke of Penthièvre, after the portrait by Hyacinthe Rigaud in 1708 (Rambouillet, Town Hall).

A prince's residence

The Count of Toulouse (1706-1737)

Louis Alexandre de Bourbon, Count of Toulouse, the legitimised son of Louis XIV and Madame de Montespan, was governor and royal lieutenant general of Brittany. Like his father, he was a keen hunter and was tempted by the domain of Rambouillet. Fleuriau d'Armenonville had little choice but to sell it to him in 1706. But he was generously rewarded, obtaining a price of 500,000 *livres*, along with the office of captain of the royal hunt at the Boulogne wood and tenure of the chateau of Madrid. According to Saint-Simon, the Count of Toulouse spent his whole life 'making Rambouillet a prodigious place.' He purchased properties in the vicinity of the chateau, ending up with 13,000 hectares of woodlands, which provided him with sizeable revenues. Incorporating Saint-Léger, Montfort and its forest, Gazeran and a large portion of the duchy of Épernon, the territory of the marquisate was doubled in surface. As well as grand admiral, the Count of Toulouse was also master of the royal hunt. To have buildings in keeping with the dignity of this office, he undertook the enlargement of the outbuildings, subsequently known as 'corridors', to house stables on the ground floor with dwellings above for the hunt officers. The kitchens were joined to the chateau by an underground passage. In August 1707, *Le Mercure galant* enthused about the elegance of the new buildings: 'There were two hundred horses with magnificent cloths […] The number of horses, all lined up with ribbons knotting their manes, the curtains at all the casements […], seen at a single glance, the whole view produces a most admirable effect.'

A royal building site

Between 1706 and 1709, the first modifications were carried out on the chateau itself. The moats were filled in and the north-west wing was altered or even entirely rebuilt. Its angled façade, on the garden side, comprised a magnificent flight of stairs, in the form of a horseshoe, visible on the 18th-century plans. At the same time the façades on the courtyard side were harmonised. The central pavilion, with curving walls on either side of the entrance, was of stone and brick. It opened onto the ground floor through a loggia, in the middle of which stood a sculpture. The two wings enclosing the courtyard were given regular bays, three storeys high, including the upper floor with its dormer windows. The courtyard was closed off by railings. For a long time, Robert de Cotte was thought to be the architect of these transformations but recent research has discovered their real authors. The King's architect Pierre Cailleteau, known as 'The Assurance', and Desgots, called Legoux, were responsible for the plans, whilst the work was supervised by the architects Jean Sarda (who styled himself 'architect to his Royal Highness the Count of Toulouse') and the lesser known Michel Jumel.

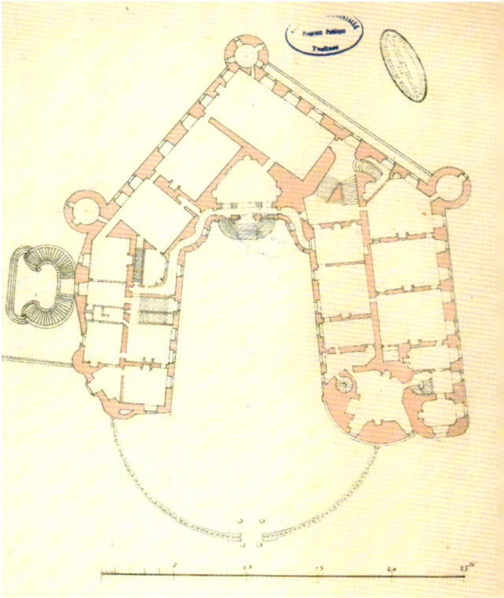

Plan of the chateau towards the middle of the18th century (Versailles, Archives départementales of the Yvelines). To the left, the wing facing the town, completed in 1707, is particularly remarkable for its curving façade and its horseshoe staircase. The wing to the right shows how the building facing the canal was doubled, in 1736, to accommodate the new Assembly apartments.

Elevation of the chateau, seen from the entrance courtyard, between 1707 and 1730 (Paris, BNF. Est. Phot.).

In August 1707, when the first phase of the modernisation of the building was almost complete, the Grand Dauphin, the Duke and Duchess of Bourgogne, the Princess of Conti and numerous courtiers came to visit Rambouillet. A contemporary gazette recounted their stay in 'the apartments of this delicious and superbly furnished residence [...] The princes and princesses stayed in the main building and all those who accompanied them in the newly-built wing, where all the apartments have been panelled in wood.'

A father's favours

By letters-patent of May 1717, the King raised the domain of Rambouillet to the status of duchy-peerage: 'In favour of our son, to give him new marks of the tenderness and satisfaction we feel for his ardent zeal in our service and his attachment to our person, marks which will pass on to posterity.' In

order to see just how splendidly his son was installed, the monarch came to Rambouillet twice, accompanied by Madame de Maintenon. If we are to believe one of the latter's comments, during her stay at the chateau in 1714, the place was delightful: 'We are swept up in pleasures from morning to night; hunts every day, often with the fleshing of the hounds right under my windows; music every evening. Our princesses are even more robust than our men of war and strengthen their liberty, which is considerable, with the air of the countryside.'

Louis XIV by Charles Le Brun, 1694,
and to his right, **Madame de Maintenon** by Pierre Mignard, 1694 (Versailles, Musée et Domaine national de Versailles et Trianon).

After the death of Louis XIV, in 1715, the Count of Toulouse was ousted from the Regency council and retired to Rambouillet. In 1723 he married Marie Victoire Sophie de Noailles, by whom he had a son, the Duke of Penthièvre, born in 1725. These family events encouraged him to pursue the improvements to his domain. The major alteration, carried out between 1730 and 1736 and giving the building its allures of a princely residence of the 18th century, was the doubling of the west wing in order to create a new suite of rooms known as the 'Assembly apartments'. This second campaign was directed by the architect Desgots, who retained the initial architectural plan. To maintain a balance between the façades, he changed the place of one of the corner turrets, which was rebuilt, then ran a balcony along the whole façade, reproducing an architectural style, which was already somewhat dated.

To the left, the balcony running along the façade of the Assembly apartments.

The refinement of the interior decors

If the outside appearance of the chateau is not particularly inventive, the same cannot be said of the interior decoration. It is from this period that dates the profusion of wooden panelling inside the chateau, still in place today and carved with exquisite delicacy.

It is attributed to Jacques Verberckt and François-Antoine Vassé, the latter the Count's favourite sculptor-ornamentist, who worked for many years at his Paris residence, the Hôtel de la Vrillière. The accounts for the work at Rambouillet have recently been studied: joinery and wood sculpture are the most costly items, an indication of their quality.

Acis and Galatea by Louis Boulogne the Elder (Tours, Musée des Beaux-Arts).

An inventory drawn up in 1718 gives some idea of the opulence of the chateau's furnishings. In particular, they show that the so-called 'King's apartments' had remarkable overdoor panels, kept today at the Museum of Tours. The themes are of course classical ones: *Diane hunting*, *Diane resting*, both painted by Louis Boulogne the Younger in 1707; *Acis and Galatea*, *The Triumph of Amphitrite*, *The Cow Io*, *The Rape of Persephone*, by Boulogne the Elder, *The Sacrifice of Bacchus*, by Michel Corneille. A tapestry depicting the history of the King of China, produced at the Beauvais manufactory and given to her son by Madame de Montespan, also decorated the walls.

Bathroom: detail of one of the panels decorated with vases and bouquets of flowers. Several birds also feature in the composition; here, in the foreground, a heron and a cock.

(Unless mentioned otherwise, the illustrations presented here come from the collections of the chateau.)

On the ground floor a bathroom was installed, a relatively rare luxury at the time but becoming more frequent during the next century. Decorated in faience, it is a masterpiece of refinement.

The Count of Toulouse died after an operation in December 1737, but Louis XV, who appreciated the company of the Countess, continued to visit Rambouillet.

Jacques Verberckt : a goldsmith's talent

In his *Discours sur la nécessité de l'étude de l'architecture* published in 1754, a treatise on the usefulness of architectural studies, Jacques François Blondel said of Jacques Verberckt that he 'knew how to bring enchantment to our homes and to our visits.'

Detail of woodwork in the president's study: cascading musical instruments, farm work.

Jacques Verberckt (1704-1771) was born in Antwerp. He served his apprenticeship with his uncle, working on the sculptures of the city's cathedral. From 1727, as sculptor and ornamentist, he belonged to the prestigious team working for the firm responsible for the King's buildings in France. In collaboration with other workshops, he developed a novel decorative style for applied woodwork. He participated in the decorative work undertaken at Versailles under Louis XV. The use of sculpted wooden panelling became widespread from the end of the 17th century, replacing the mural paintings and arabesques of the preceding century in royal palaces and princely residences. For many contemporaries, the delicacy of this type of decor made it comparable to the art of the goldsmith. From 1720 to 1740 Verberckt, still at the beginning of his career, was one of the leading figures in the emergence of the Rococo style, characteristic of the decorative arts under the Regency and Louis XV. His manner, which art historians describe as the 'rich style', can be distinguished by the attention given to the surrounding mouldings as much as to the panels' contents. The apartments of the Countess of Toulouse are amongst the most splendid examples of this type of decor.

The Duke of Penthièvre, portrait attributed to Jean-Baptiste Charpentier, painter to the Duke's household, 18th century (Rambouillet, Town Hall).

The Duke of Penthièvre: surprises in an English garden (1737-1783)

Louis Jean-Marie de Bourbon, Duke of Penthièvre (1725-1793), the son of the Count of Toulouse and of Marie Victoire Sophie de Noailles, was born at Rambouillet. The domain became his favourite place of residence. His main contribution there lies in the composition of the gardens. He developed the network of water features, creating two secondary canals, spreading in a fan pattern along former avenues. These canals created a series of islands, left as meadows, apart from two which, judging from Rigaud's engraving , were covered with copses.

The Duke of Penthièvre's family in 1768, or *The Cup of Chocolate*, portraits of the Duke and his son, the Prince of Lamballe and the latter's wife, by Jean-Baptiste Charpentier the Elder (Versailles, Musée et Domaine national de Versailles et Trianon).

The canals, engraving by Rigaud, perspective seen from the Assembly apartments during the period of the Duke of Penthièvre's occupation (Paris, BNF. Est. Phot.).

The shell cottage, engraving after Georges Louis Le Rouge.

Such formal gardens *à la française*, in the French manner, were still appreciated during the second half of the 18th century but the truly up-to-date ones were the so-called *jardins à l'anglaise*, in the English style. The Duke of Penthièvre commissioned a landscape designer – his name has yet to be discovered – to conceive a garden of this sort at Rambouillet, covering twenty-five hectares in the undulating part of the park between the canals and the forest. A network of sinuous alleys and a serpentine river, crossed over by little bridges or by stepping-stones, led the visitor towards mysterious folly-type buildings intended to provoke emotions of surprise or to serve as invitations for meditation. Constructed between 1770 and 1780 by Jean-

Baptiste Paindebeld, 'contractor and architect of English gardens', under the direction of the Duke's architect, Claude Martin Goupy, the shell cottage, the hermitage and the Chinese pavilion all illustrate the new repertoire that began to emerge after 1760, mingling exoticism and vernacular styles. The first two structures, covered with thatched roofs, are exemplary of the contemporary taste for the picturesque, rustic style. From outside, they offer an idealised image of a peasant's dwelling, whilst inside they provide the exquisite comfort expected by Rambouillet's prestigious visitors. The most famous example of this architectural genre, the Queen's hamlet at Versailles, was built some time later, between 1783 and 1787. The hermitage was constructed on a craggy summit in the park known as the Coudray heights, overlooking the estate. The structure was damaged by fire in 1977 but restoration work has recently commenced. Comprising several rooms, it differs from other, simpler hermitages built in parks of the time in the fact that it includes a chapel. Sometimes these hermitages were peopled by real hermits or by a mechanical automaton!

A swing at Rambouillet, engraving after Georges Louis Le Rouge, from *Jardins anglo-chinois à la mode,* 1776-1789, a publication on fashionable Anglo-Chinese gardens.

The tradition of shell decoration

The nymphaeum or grotto of the chateau of Wideville (Yvelines)

The drinking trough of the stables at the chateau of Maisons, Maisons-Laffitte (Yvelines).

The decoration of the shell cottage at Rambouillet is a late expression of a tradition of Italian origin, adopted in France during the second half of the 16th century. The royal chateaux encouraged such creations, in particular at the pine grotto at Fontainebleau (Seine-et-Marne) or in the grottoes of the new chateau of Saint-Germain-en-Laye (Yvelines). These celebrated examples having since been lost, it is in the Loire department, at the chateau of the Bastie d'Urfé, that one of the oldest surviving examples of this type of shell decoration is to be seen today. In 1548, commissioned by Claude d'Urfé, two refreshment rooms, called grottoes, were decorated with ornamental panels and figures studded with sea-shells, concretions and coloured stones. In the Île-de-France region, several other sites also used shells in their garden structures: the chateaux of Leyrit at Auvers-sur-Oise (Val d'Oise), of Viry-Châtillon (Essonne) and of Wideville (Yvelines) where the famous nymphaeum or grotto of 1635 is decorated with panels of shells and multi-coloured crystals. Mention may also be made of the 1650 drinking trough at the main stables of the chateau of Maisons-Laffitte (Yvelines), incorporated today into a 19th-century house.

It should be noted, however, that unlike the cottage at Rambouillet, all these earlier structures are associated with water and the notion of freshness, and that the sea-shells are mingled freely with other rustic materials like millstone concretions or cinders. The example at Rambouillet, one of the last, stands out as the most refined in terms of the quality and delicacy of its design.

Detail of the shell incrustation at the cottage at Rambouillet. The decorative shells are fixed to the wall with the aid of tinted mortar and tiny nails.

A royal chateau

Louis XVI (1783-1789)

Louis XVI by Antoine François Callet, 1776 (private collection).

Louis XV often came to hunt in the Yvelines forest. For his accommodation during these outings, and in order to avoid imposing on his cousin the Duke of Penthièvre, he had the chateau of Saint-Hubert built not far from Rambouillet, close to the lakes of Pourras. Jacques Ange Gabriel was the architect of this new residence, built between 1755 and 1759. But Louis XVI, also a frequent visitor to the region on account of its rich stock of game, was no longer satisfied with the residence at Saint-Hubert, finding it too 'poky'. He insisted to the Duke of Penthièvre that he desired to acquire the domain of Rambouillet and Penthièvre could but accede to this royal pressure, selling the domain to the King for sixteen million *livres* in 1783. Louis XVI acquired the domain privately, wanting to pass his time there not as the monarch but as the Lord of Rambouillet, doing as he wished on the estate 'without all the meetings and confusions of the Crown estate commissioners.' The chateau of Saint-Hubert was neglected and gradually fell into ruin; it was demolished in 1855.

View of the chateau of Saint-Hubert by Thomas Compigne, 18th century (Sceaux, Musée de l'Île-de-France). Louis XVI's acquisition of the chateau of Rambouillet caused the ruin of these buildings.

A bucolic court

Charles Claude Flahaut de La Billarderie, the Count d'Angiviller, a cavalry officer, was appointed by the King as governor of his domain at Rambouillet, where the construction of an entirely new chateau was envisaged. Several projects were presented by Jean Augustin Renard, architect and controller of the King's buildings, but the site was not large enough to allow for a harmonious composition and in the end it was decided to keep the existing buildings. Two months after the purchase, Louis XVI commissioned the architect Jacques Jean Thévenin to undertake major works, directed by the contractor Delanoue. This operation was on a considerable scale, sometimes occupying as many as nine hundred workers at a time! Stone quarries were opened at Gazeran and at Saint-Hilarion, a brick works installed at Mocquesouris and plaster works and lime kilns erected on the site itself. All this activity was required primarily for the enlargement of the Count of Toulouse's stable buildings in order to provide the facilities necessary for the lifestyle of the domain's new, royal master. The façades were re-appointed in order to give them a semblance of unity. It was also necessary to construct a new stable building, known as the 'small stables', accommodating the cavalry headquarters and no fewer than five hundred horses! New buildings were also erected in the town, a governor's building, a bailiff's court and a building for the royal hunt, as well as a town house for the Count d'Angivillier himself, replaced a few decades later by the palace of the King of Rome.

The chateau and its main outbuildings, etching after Basire, 1787 (Sceaux, Musée de l'Île-de-France). These outbuildings could accommodate up to four hundred servants.

The dairy

Marie-Antoinette found Rambouillet boring and 'gothic'. In the hope that she might appreciate the place better, her husband ordered the construction of a sumptuous dairy in the park, built in secret. Hidden behind a palisade of branches, it was revealed to the Queen and the court in June 1787.

Marie-Antoinette, by Élisabeth Louise Vigée-Lebrun, 1783 (Darmstadt, Chateau Museum).

The ornamental or hygienic dairy

During the reign of Louis XVI, dairies and shepherdesses were all the rage. In his 1832 *Dictionnaire historique d'architecture*, under the heading *Laiterie* [Dairy], Quatremere de Quincy wrote: 'In country houses, where wealthy people pursue rustic occupations, the dairy is an amenity [...] where light meals may be served. A fountain is often installed, offering coolness during the heat of the summer [...]. The most remarkable dairy of this sort is the one at the royal chateau of Rambouillet.'

During the 18th century, a distinction was made between the ornamental dairy, also called the 'hygienic' or 'pleasure' dairy, and the real dairy for milking cows and preparing cream, butter and cheese, known as a 'utility' dairy. The return to nature recommended in the writings of Jean-Jacques Rousseau was one of the influences in this fashion for ornamental dairies, although a few 17th-century dairies existed before his time. Louis XIV, for example, had a dairy built in his menagerie at Versailles.

During the 18th century, in crown properties, dairies were to be found at Louis XVI's chateau of Saint-Cloud, at the Duke d'Orléans' chateau at Raincy and at the Duke de Condé's chateau at Chantilly. The best known dairy, however, was the one built for Marie-Antoinette at Versailles by Richard Mique from 1782 to 1784. Such ornamental dairies often feature amongst the different folly-like buildings erected in other new parks during the 18th century.

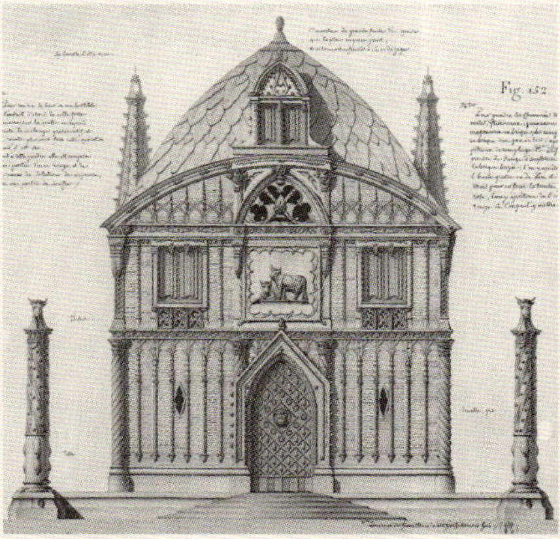

Dairy designed by the architect Lequeu, late 18th century (Paris, BNF, Est. Phot.).

The dairy at Versailles.

Hubert Robert, the King's painter and gardener

The King asked Hubert Robert to provide the setting for the dairy and to redesign the gardens. This artist, 'designer of the King's gardens', had already conceived the new baths of Apollo at Versailles in 1781. He was a friend of the King whom he had frequented since his youth when he was a gentleman-in-waiting at the chambers of the royal children. Robert arranged the dairy and its ancillary buildings inside a vast enclosed space where an English-style garden was created, planted with exotic trees. The fashion at the time was to mix domestic trees with now-acclimatised exotic ones, imported from America or elsewhere. An 'English' river was lined with Carolina wax-trees, pyramid oaks, spruces, Atlas and

Hubert Robert by Élisabeth Louise Vigée-Lebrun, 1788 (Paris, Musée du Louvre).

La Fête à Rambouillet or L'Île de l'amour by Fragonard, 1770 (Lisbon, Calouste Gulbenkian Foundation). This painting of a fête at Rambouillet, also known as 'The Island of Love', is a theatrical evocation of the place rather than a realistic image. It gives a good idea of the mingled sentiments of fear and delight that Hubert Robert aimed to provoke in certain spots in the park.

Lebanese cedars, Chinese thuyas, copper beeches, robinias and sweet gum trees. The King followed the project closely and participated in the design. He asked Robert to enlarge the English garden created for the Duke of Penthièvre and to soften the lines of the regular garden by creating some circular alleys planted with acacias. He wanted bowers to be planted around the water features, 'all different, each one composed of the same variety of fruit tree', thereby creating sizeable orchards. A 1788 guide for visitors to Paris mentioned these orchards: 'Roads of varied fruit trees of the best species, a few clumps of flowering shrubs or fruit-bearing bushes set on large expanses of lawn, flowers mingled amidst these plantations, no straight lines in the alleys which all wind along simply… this is how this charming orchard is composed.'

Branch of a pear tree, with dragonfly, botanical plate by Barbara Regina, mid-18th century (Warwickshire, USA, Museum of Fine Arts).

The experimental farm

If the dairy at Rambouillet was part of bucolic court protocol created for the amusement of the Queen, Louis XVI's desire to set up a sheep farm there was

Alexandre Henri Tessier (1746-1837), a life devoted to sheep

Alexandre Henri Tessier (Paris, BNF, Est. Phot.)
Tessier was a doctor of medicine, regent of the faculty of medicine in Paris, Knight of the Order of Saint-Michel, member of the Legion of Honour, general inspector of the National Sheep Farm and member of the *Institut français* from 1795. During his lifetime, he enjoyed considerable renown.

Member of the Royal Society of Medicine and a reputed agronomist, Alexandre Henri Tessier devoted his life to sheep breeding and agricultural experiments. His scientific capacities were recognised by all and whatever the regime – monarchy, republic or empire – he remained the expert in the development of merino sheep farming. Drawing on the conclusions of Daubenton, he accommodated the Spanish flock in a provisional pen installed at the bleaching house of Mocquesouris. In 1794 he opened a highly successful school for shepherds, claiming that its graduates were 'the leading shepherds of France'. Amongst other experiments carried out on the 275 hectares put at his disposal, he carried out trials on the planting of wheat using a dibble, a device recently imported from England. He also studied the culture of wheat and the seeding of exotic plants. The Revolutionary authorities did not contest his competence or the economic interest of his research. A report on the sheep station dated 7 Ventôse Year IV (26 February 1796) concluded that 'after nine years of experimentation, the wool of this precious flock and its improvement [...] lead us to consider the establishment at Rambouillet as an object of the greatest importance [...], a conquest which can lead to the elimination of Spanish wool by the regeneration of French wools. It would be a shame to abandon the fruits of this work [...]. It is in the national interest to conserve, protect, improve and develop as far as possible the rural establishment in the Rambouillet park.' Napoleon was also conscious of the importance of this breeding centre and it was he who had the present-day station built, still under the direction of Tessier. Tessier was a doctor, regent of the Paris faculty of medicine, general inspector of sheep farms and a member of the Institute. He made considerable contributions to the modernisation of French agriculture. It is thanks to his initiative that the sheep farm is today the national genetic conservatory for the Rambouillet breed of merino sheep.

National Sheep Farm, engraving, early 19th century (Paris, BNF. Est. Phot.).

inspired rather by scientific and economic considerations. As early as 1766, Louis Daubenton, keeper of the collections at the royal gardens in Paris and a former collaborator of Buffon, had already begun some experiments at Montbard on merino sheep. The aim of these experiments was to improve France's woollen cloth industry, the cloth made with indigenous wools being of inferior quality to products made of Spanish merino wools. When the King acquired Rambouillet, Malesherbes and d'Angiviller (who was associated with the French Academy of Science) suggested that he pursue the experiments. A flock of merino sheep left Segovia on 13 June 1786 and crossed the kingdom to reach Rambouillet on 12 October, accompanied by its Spanish shepherds. The flock was comprised of forty-two rams, three hundred and thirty-four ewes and seven 'leader sheep' along with the requisite sheepdogs. Alexandre Henri Tessier was appointed to run the sheep farm and the important agricultural centre that completed it. The farm buildings, located in the upper part of the park beyond the valley, formed part of the new gardens designed by Hubert Robert.

Merino rams born at Rambouillet sixteen years after their importation in 1786 (Archives de la Bergerie nationale).

Flock of merino sheep in the Allée de Montorgeuil at Rambouillet (Bergerie nationale).

Napoleon I

Imperial renaissance (1804-1815)

Napoleon I by Andrea Appiani in 1807 (Vienna, Museum of Art and History). The Emperor is represented here as the King of Italy.

During the Revolution, the domain of Rambouillet was abandoned, but since it was part of Louis XVI's civil list, it also became a property of the First Consul. According to statistics compiled by certain historians, Napoleon spent some sixty days at Rambouillet, which, considering his exceptional mobility, is worthy of note. He too appreciated the pleasures of the hunt and was responsible for stocking the forest at Rambouillet with deer from the Black Forest.

As at all his residences, the Emperor undertook major works at Rambouillet. In 1805, the architect he had commissioned, Guillaume Trepsat, took the radical step of demolishing the left wing enclosing the central courtyard, which completely broke the general equilibrium of the chateau. After this disaster, a complete reconstruction was envisaged in 1809. The architect August Famin, a Prix de Rome winner, drew up several projects, but none were executed. Instead, inside the partly mutilated building, the circulation was reorganised, with the creation of a double flight of stairs and a new façade fronting the main building. A passage was opened through the tower in order to connect the apartments there with those on the first floor. Decoration work was undertaken, in particular for a sumptuous bathroom for the Emperor.

Plan of the ground floor of Rambouillet, first quarter of the 19th century (Paris, Archives nationales). The left wing has been demolished (see plan on p. 9).

From 1807, the English garden was also the object of a thoroughgoing transformation: tombstones, antique-style monuments, numerous statues borrowed from what was known as the 'special Museum of the French school at Versailles' and various garden buildings (since destroyed) were installed by the architect Famin. Trees were replanted too, including the famous *allée* of black Louisiana cypresses, unique in France at the time and blown down by the tempest of 1999. The buildings in the 18th-century garden were restored and the bridges, stepping stones and decorative piles of millstone along the English river♦ were repaired. Special attention was paid to the dairy which the Emperor wanted to offer to his new wife Marie-Louise, suggesting the importance that the Emperor attached to such vestiges of the *Ancien Régime*. For Napoleon's own use, a new hunting lodge was also built. Famin was responsible for overseeing these operations, restocking the canals with fish, looking after the gondolas and rowing boats and bringing forty couples of swans from the chateau of Laeken in Belgium. The swans were delivered by parcel post!

The 'English' river

If hunting brought the Emperor to Rambouillet, the sheep farm was another preoccupation, because the merino sheep were vital for the prosperity of the national wool trade. The farm was rebuilt and proper accommodation at last provided for the precious animals. The Emperor is said to have observed 'Spain has twenty-five million merino sheep; I want France to have a hundred million.'

But on 22 June 1815, after Waterloo, Napoleon abdicated, one of his last nights on French soil being spent at Rambouillet.

♦***'English' river or rivière anglaise:*** *river situated in a garden landscaped in the English manner, after the fashion which appeared in France during the 18th century. Unlike the ornamental canals of French-style gardens, an English river always has a sinuous course.*

View of the redesigned gardens by the architect Famin. Plate from Alexandre de Laborde's *Description des nouveaux jardins de la France…*, 1808.

A neglected chateau

When Louis XVIII came to the throne in 1815, the chateau was again refurbished. The work involved the eradication all traces of the Empire. The façade overlooking the canal was altered, but only three of the planned arched windows were realised before the work was interrupted, once again compromising the unity of the chateau's appearance. Succeeding his brother, Charles X mounted the throne on 16 September 1824. The new monarch hunted at Rambouillet, but the most significant episode linking him to the chateau was his abdication on 2 August 1830, in favour of his grandson the Duke of Bordeaux. This took place in the hall of the chateau, the present-day dining room. Charles X then left for exile in England. The chateau was then

Charles X in his coronation splendour, by François Gérard, 1824 (Versailles, Musée et Domaine national de Versailles et Trianon).

entrusted to the administration of the crown properties, losing much of its splendour. King Louis-Philippe did not keep it on his civil list and it was let out to various occupants: Baron Schikler, the Count Duchatel. It was even transformed for a while into a luxurious restaurant and gentleman's club. In 1852, the chateau entered the civil list again and was used by Napoleon III for rest and for state meetings. After the fall of the Empire in 1870, the chateau was neglected again. The administration envisaged various uses for the site, including its conversion into a hospital. This was refused by Thiers, however, who said it would be vandalism.

Jacques Chirac, President of the Republic, with Nelson Mandela at Rambouillet, 13 July 1996.

A presidential residence

A hunting venue for the heads of the French state,1883-1995

From 1883 on, the presidents of the Republic resumed the traditional hunts at Rambouillet. Jules Grévy, Sadi Carnot and Jean Casimir-Perier all appreciated the venue and a new hunting lodge was built for Grévy in 1886. Jacques Chirac put an end to the presidential hunts in 1995, but hunting still takes place at Rambouillet. Every year the administration invites the men and women who have received the highest marks in the exam to acquire a hunting licence.

It was from 1895, under President Félix Faure, that Rambouillet also became a place for summer retreats and was transformed into a presidential residence. The furniture comes from the *Mobilier national*, the national furniture collections. Some pieces remain in place whilst others come and go according to fashion and the tastes of succeeding presidents. Since they have been opened to the public, the furniture arrangement of the Assembly apartments has become permanent. In the François I tower, only open to the public on special occasions, the decoration, dating from the early 1950s under President Vincent Auriol, is by the well-known creator Jules Leleu.

The sculpted decoration in the park has also witnessed changes. A recent work, commissioned by the Ministry of Culture during François Mitterrand's second term of office, was erected in 1993. Entitled the *Solar Boat*, it was sculpted by Karel and installed at the centre of the quincunx.

The *Solar Boat* by Karel; sculpture founded by Prazin in 1992 at the Coubertin foundry.

Visit

The main courtyard

The main courtyard is now made up of the two surviving façades of the chateau, set at right angles to each other. It is closed off by ornamental railings set on top of a low wall forming a semi-circle. To the right, the so-called François I tower with its battlements and machicolations forms an imposing mass even though it is integrated into the volumes built during the 18th century.

The façades of the two main buildings were harmonised during the 19th century. The north façade at the end of the courtyard, flanked by a small turret with a pepper-pot roof, was built by the architect Trepsat in 1805 after the demolition of the left wing which extended to the gatehouse. At the end of the courtyard, a perron and a monumental doorway form the main entrance to the chateau.

View towards the main courtyard. From right to left, the Assembly apartments, completed in 1736, the 14th-century tower known as the François I tower, and the entrance wing, redesigned by Famin from 1809.

The façades facing the garden

The most homogeneous façade, presenting a regular succession of windows crowned by brick pediments and dormers, is that of the so-called 'Assembly apartments' built for the Count of Toulouse. A balcony with a splendid 18th-century wrought-iron balustrade runs along its whole length. The façade facing the grand canal (where the floor levels do not coincide with those of the main building) is framed by two turrets topped with pepper-pot roofs. The different architectural styles are slightly disconcerting and result from two interventions by the architect Famin, the first under the Empire and the second under Louis XVIII. In the first campaign, the windows were decorated with classical pediments and underlined by a balcony with neo-classical ironwork. This balcony is continued along the third façade and connects the Emperor's apartments with those of the Empress. During the second campaign, this façade was again embellished by the opening up of large windows with rounded arches, framed by Doric pilasters supporting a projecting band and overhanging cornice. Of the six windows planned, only three were in fact realised, in about 1820. These windows brought generous light to the dining room, aligned with the canal. In this unfinished state of affairs, the only unifying feature for the façade as a whole is the cornice under the roof,

with its alternating metopes and triglyphs.♦ The third façade, similarly framed by two pepper-pot turrets, gives on to the flower beds. This façade also differs from the two others in its flat bands at the cornice level and in the presence of an intermediary level between the first and top floors. A visit to the place is always a surprise, on account of the rather severe exterior appearance of the chateau contrasting with the astonishing variety of ornamental styles inside. The visit commences by one of the two grand flights of stairs, built under Napoleon.

♦***Metopes and triglyphs:*** *these constitute the frieze of the Doric order. The triglyph comprises three concave mouldings whilst the metope is a square supporting element, often decorated with sculpted motifs.*

Perspective view of the chateau: to the left, the façade opening onto the grand canal; to the right, the façade giving on to the flower bed of the *rondeau*.

The richness of the interior decoration

The Renaissance staircase[4]

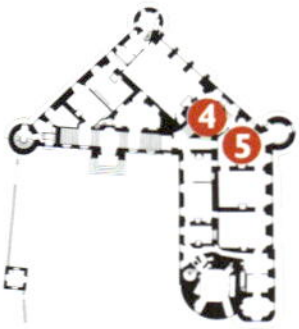

First floor

This staircase is one of the few remaining architectural elements dating from the 16th century. Its ceiling, with its curved and groined brick vaulting, is characteristic of staircase designs in French Renaissance buildings. The stairs lead up to the first floor and to a vestibule which opens out onto the suite of rooms which constitute the Assembly apartments. Collectively, these represent a masterpiece of French 18th-century decorative work, still conserved *in situ*.
The oak panels, delicately sculpted with foliated scrolls, festoons and intertwining volutes, conserve a clarity and symmetry of frames which are characteristic of Rococo art.

The Assembly apartments

The Meridian salon[5]

This room serves as an antechamber to the Assembly apartments, although it was perhaps used as a dining room during the 18th century. This would seem to be suggested by the iconography of the decorative woodwork and the cornices: the dominant theme is the vine. Above the niche, in the corner of the room, the sculpted decor associates a bunch of grapes, the emblem

of Dionysus, with ears of corn and baskets of fruit tumbling in a spray held together with ribbons. In the recess, the stove in white varnished faience harmonises perfectly with the room's decoration. Originally, however, it came from the city of Rheims which offered it as a gift to President Coty during his presidency (1953-1959).

The central table dates from the reign of Louis-Philippe (1830-1848).
On the mantelpiece above the fireplace, the clock in gilded bronze, in the Louis XVI style, is the work of the Parisian clock-smith Courvoisier.

Faïence stove,
18th-century,
and fireplace.

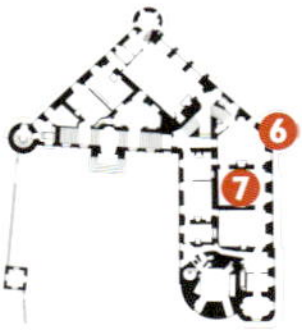

First floor

The Oratory[6]

The oratory opens on to the Meridian salon. It was created for the Duke of Penthièvre inside the south-west turret. The Bishop of Chartres gave it his blessing on 31 July 1772. It was subsequently redecorated for the Empress Marie-Louise but its present-day appearance dates from restoration work carried out under Louis XVIII. The coffered ceiling and the pilasters are painted in *trompe-l'œil*, the latter decorated with censers, pontifical tiaras or bishops' mitres, and also with medallions bearing the royal fleur-de-lis and the King's monogram. The band around the upper section of the ceiling bears the Latin inscription: 'Lord, you send us now your servant. According to thy word, it is in peace that my eyes shall see thy salvation.' In front of the altar, the prayer-stools in gilded wood date from the Empire whilst the altar cross and the chandeliers are of the Restoration period. The altar itself is draped with brocade and so-called Indian silk, a striped fabric produced in the workshops of Lyons and much appreciated during the Empire. The two Medici vases in Sèvres porcelain, with floral decorations, date from the middle of the 19th century.

The Council Chamber[7]

It was during the presidency of Félix Faure (1896-1899) that the council of ministers began to convene at Rambouillet while the president was staying there. This salon thus earned its name as the Council Chamber. It is in fact the first of the five rooms which comprise the Assembly apartments built for the Count of Toulouse. Its wooden panelling is remarkable and the quality gets better throughout these apartments. Recent research has been able to attribute the execution of this panelling to Jacques Verberckt and François Antoine Vassé. This particular room is dedicated to one of the former mistresses of the domain, Marie Victoire Sophie de Noailles, the wife of the Count of Toulouse who commissioned the work. The mark of the young lady, in delicate traceries sometimes done in tiny flowers, decorates the panels and the cornice. Two mirrors multiply the effects of these sculpted panels.

Two of the twelve Louis XV armchairs, in polished beech.

The Hare and the Tortoise, The Fox and the Stork, details of the embroidery on the seats of the armchairs.

Geography and Astronomy, overdoor panel painting.

During the 19th century, Marie Félix Hippolyte-Lucas painted the overdoor panels with scenes evoking the sciences and the arts. *Geography and Astronomy* shows Atlas carrying the terrestrial globe and an armillary or celestial sphere symbolising these two sciences. The presence of the pomegranates, the clock, the upturned ewer and jewellery also make of this work an allusion to the vanity of life. The Gobelins tapestry was woven by Cozette *fils* in 1791, after a cartoon by François Boucher. The two medallions are decorated with mythological scenes: *Venus emerging from the Waves* and *Psyche contemplating Love*

A pheasant featuring above the signature of the tapestry weaver Cozette *fils*, detail of the Gobelins tapestry.

Psyche contemplating Love Asleep, detail of one of the medallions of the Gobelins tapestry.

Asleep. The furniture is comprised of twelve armchairs and a sofa dating from the reign of Louis XV, all covered in fine-pointed Flemish tapestry. The seats illustrate fables by La Fontaine, *The Hare and the Tortoise* and *The Fox and the Stork*, amongst others. The backs of the chairs are decorated with rustic or amorous scenes.

The presidential study[8]

The woodwork panelling presents gracious sprays of tumbling objects which evoke music, hunting, gardening and farm work, following the seasons at the chateau during the time of the Count of Toulouse. Lute, parasol, hat, hunting horn, quiver with arrows, ears of corn, flowers, hunting net, basket of fruit, bow and arrow, rake, spade, watering can, horn of abundance, pears, flail, sickle, boar's head, hunting guns, torches… taken together, these objects offer a complete vocabulary of early 18th-century decorative motifs.

Poseidon and Amphitrite on a Sea Chariot, accompanied by sea nymphs, overdoor panel representing *Fishing.*

First floor

The overdoor panels by Hippolyte-Lucas, commissioned by President Félix Faure in 1899, occupy the frames of the original paintings that the Duke of Penthièvre had taken to his chateau of Chanteloup. The scenes evoke hunting, fishing, the dawn and repose, all symbolised by the 'agreeable nudes' characteristic of the late-19th-century *pompier* or official Beaux-Arts style. The main salon is furnished with an ensemble upholstered in yellow damask, dating from the reign of Louis XV, signed by N. Nadal, D. Decant, F. Foliot and J. Brocsolle.

The next three rooms are smaller than this salon and characterise the tendency that emerged during the first half of the 18th century to multiply such small rooms, corresponding with a new taste for intimacy.

Diana surrounded by her Nymphs, overdoor panel evoking *The Hunt.*

Antechamber[9]

The wooden panelling of this room is slightly different in its design. The panels are arranged on four levels and their decoration of rosettes is simpler. Two doors are hidden in the panelling, one leading to a secret staircase that goes down to the ground-floor bathroom, the other joining up with the apartments facing the courtyard.

The small salon[10]

For a long time, this salon was occupied by a library which was moved under Valéry Giscard d'Estaing. It is now decorated with a large 18th-century tapestry from the Aubusson works and entitled *The Boar Hunt*. The dimensions of this salon also bear witness to the new fashion for private spaces for more intimate gatherings, preferred to larger state chambers.

The rich Rococo decoration here recalls that of the Queen's bedroom at Versailles of 1730.

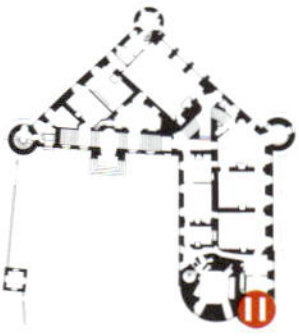

First floor

The boudoir[11]

In this room, known as 'Marie-Antoinette's boudoir' or the 'turret cabinet of the Queen's apartment', Rambouillet's demonstration of the ornamentist's art reaches its apogee. Writing in the mid-20th century, the art historian Louis Hautecœur described the carved decoration as forming a 'veritable gossamer-like filigree stretched out over the wood.' After 1970 the whole room was painted white. This marked a conscious return to the traditions of the 18th century, although without gold highlighting on the relief. The panels are lit by two large casement windows and a mirror. Their iconography and the delicate execution of the panelling make this circular boudoir a sort of belvedere at the end of the apartments, a world of its own.

Sagittarius and Gemini, signs of the zodiac featuring in the frieze.

Europe, Africa, America and Asia at the corners of the frieze.

In the corners, the four regions of the known world are symbolised by animals: a horse for Europe, a rhinoceros for Africa, an alligator for America and a camel for Asia. The four elements are depicted by animated scenes with little children or 'putti': putti-blacksmiths for Fire, putti-gardeners for Earth, putti frolicking in Water and, for Air, putti blowing breezes. Set in the scrolls of the frieze are the signs of the zodiac.

Water (in the centre) **and Earth** (below), two of the four elements illustrated by their respective putti. The ornamental details integrated into the arabesques surrounding these scenes underline the themes evoked: fishing nets and fish for Water, fruit and flowers for the Earth.

The Emperor's apartments

Returning through the Assembly apartments, the visitor comes to a secret door that leads to the Emperor's apartments. *The passage gives an idea of the thickness of the wall of the François I tower, integrated into the wing overlooking the courtyard.*

The triumphal arch of the Carrousel and Malmaison, medallions by Vasserot.

First floor

The bathroom12

This bathroom was created in 1807 and still retains its original painted decor and its imperial bathtub in tin-plated copper. The ornamental composition, in a latter-day version of the Pompeian style, was executed by the painter Pierre François Godard. The room is structured by pilasters supporting an architrave with metopes and triglyphs of the Doric order, a broad frieze and, above, a corona with lyres and palmettes. The decorative details, comprising delicately painted garlands, draperies, flowers and birds, are characteristic of a repertory inspired by classical antiquity, but the iconography also glorifies Napoleon's Empire: his coronation, military trophies,

an allusion to the Treaty of Amiens and to a naval battle. On the end wall, two figures of fame exalt a beehive buzzing with bees and framed by gryphons. Rich in symbols, this decor also comprises two medals of the *Légion d'Honneur*, the order founded by the Emperor in 1802.
The bees, emblems of Napoleonic heraldry, are hardly visible today but restoration work could bring them out in the background of the panels and on the pilasters. The ensemble is completed by fourteen medallions painted on canvas by Jean Vasserot between 1809 and 1810. According to tradition, the artist first depicted members of the imperial family, but the subject was not deemed appropriate for a bathroom so he covered these portraits with views of Italy (Rome, Vesuvius, etc.) and of various imperial properties (Saint-Cloud, Malmaison, the Tuileries …).
The suite of apartments includes a bedroom and a dining room giving on to the main courtyard. Their furniture dates from the Directory and Empire periods and, following the changes undertaken for different presidential visits, is regularly replaced or moved around by the curators of the state furniture collections.
A few stairs lead to the former apartments of the King, also situated on the first floor but at a slightly different level.

View from the bath: two mirrors at either end enlarge the space and multiply the luxurious decorative effects. The bathtub in tin-plated copper was manufactured by the coppersmith Chapsal who also supplied the boiler.

First floor

The main dining room[13]

During the 18th century, what today comprises this dining room and its associated pantry was the so-called King's chamber, the room affording the best view out over the grand canal. It was probably altered during the 19th century when it was used for receptions: two musicians' boxes survive at the upper end of the room.

Today this room is used as a ceremonial dining room for presidential receptions. On the walls two impressively large Gobelins tapestries depict scenes from the *New Indies*, *The Negress carried in a Hammock* and *The Indian Hunter*. These tapestries were executed by Cozette *fils* in 1792, after cartoons by Jean François Desportes. The note of exoticism provided by

Tapestry of *The Negress carried in a Hammock*.

these tapestries is complemented by five other colourful wall hangings specially produced for this room by the Beauvais manufacture between 1899 and 1901.
The cartoons, by Achille Cesbron, show a series of birds: *The Pheasant*, *The Cock*, *The Parakeet*, *The Parrot* and *The Peacock*.

A sheep, a crowned crane and the central figure beneath her parasol, details from the tapestry *The Negress carried in a Hammock*.

Tapestry of the *Indian Hunter*.

Exotic birds and reptiles, details.

The birds by Achille Cesbron, tapestries used as overdoor panels.

The monogram of the French Republic – R. F. – draws attention to the identity of the patron and owner of the property, the French State. The floor is covered with a Savonnerie carpet dating from the Second Empire and measuring about seventy square metres. Its floral motif gives a *trompe-l'œil* effect. The walls and all the Empire furniture in the room, originally in mahogany, were subsequently painted in a grey hue. The room has recently been restored and its painted decoration set off in gold leaf.

Carpet from the Savonnerie manufacture, detail.

The ground floor

On the ground floor, only two ooms are open to the public. The rest of this level, which often undergoes alterations, is reserved for presidential stays.

The Marble Room!

This is one of the oldest nteriors in the chateau, lating from 1556. The walls re covered with slabs of red nd grey Languedoc marble. Under different presidents, he room has been used variously as a billiards room, salon and a reception room. On the mantel, the bust of François I recalls his visit to the chateau. It is a copy of the bust executed in 1756 by Louis Claude Antoine Vassé, after another bust that was then at Fontainebleau. This room underwent an important restoration programme, completed in 2003.

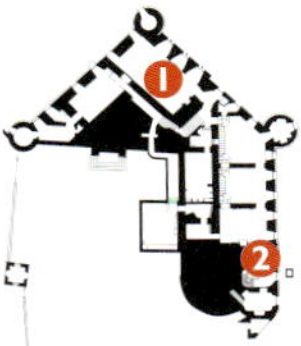

Ground floor

Marble slabs constituting panels with geometric designs.

The Faïence cabinet[2]

On account of the fragility of its decor, this room cannot be entered and is visible only from the doorway. This decor dates from the works undertaken for the Count of Toulouse between 1730 and 1736. Sometimes known as 'Marie-Antoinette's former bathroom', it is one of very few such bathrooms of the period surviving in its original context. A hidden door in the Assembly apartments gives access to this bathroom, the walls of which are entirely covered with blue Delft tiles, all of different design. This profusion of faïence is perhaps a recollection of the first Trianon palace, known as 'the porcelain Trianon', built at Versailles during the preceding century.

The two large seascapes in the Flemish manner are signed with the initials C.B.M., those of Cornelis Bou Maester. The maritime imagery is possibly a reference to the Count of Toulouse's charge as grand admiral of the fleet. The apparent coldness of these blue tiles is set off by the bright polychromy of the four panels with floral compositions which complete the decoration. Originally thought to have been produced at Rouen, they are now known to have come from Valence in Spain. The walls are crowned by a stucco cornice with decorative references to the theme of bathing: water jets, reeds, fish and sea monsters all mingled together in a Rococo frieze.

Flower vase, a detail from one of the faïence panels showing remarkable precision in the representation of the flowers and animals.

One of the seascapes.

The formal French garden

Fraternal Charity and *The Death of Procris* on the banks of the grand canal.

The canals and the flower beds

On the town side, the chateau's horizons are hemmed in. The open views are to the south, on the garden side. In front of the building, the main landing stage promises departures in small boats or gondolas, a reminder of the games of gallantry – the embarkation for Cythera, for example – in which 18th-century aristocratic society revelled. This landing stage was originally flanked by two figures *Alpheus* and *Arethusa*, sculpted by René Frémin, replaced today by two groups in marble: to the left, *The Death of Procris*, by Jean Escoula (1898) and *Fraternal Charity*, by Julien Édouard Conny (1865). Six islands punctuate the canals, two of them circular, the Banquet Island and the Rock Island. The passengers descend marble staircases framed by columns topped by spheres, dating from the Empire. During the 18th century, amidst the stone blocks of the Rock Island, there was a small octagonal temple decorated with carved woodwork. Restored during the Empire, it has since been demolished. Amongst the 18th-century flower beds, the only one to survive today is the lime-tree quincunx. Amidst these trees, there is a pillar known as a Herm pillar, bearing

A landing stage on the grand canal.

a sculpted head, originally of Hermes, the god of travellers. The pillar at Rambouillet has a sculpted head of Aesculapius and is the last survivor of a series of nineteen such pillars. The most recent work to enter the domain, Karel's *Solar Boat*, was placed here in 1993. To the south of the town, the garden has been restored since 1995 by the landscape gardener Jacques Sgard. The 'grand copse', the 'mirror', the 'little copse' and the '*rondeau*' offer a 20th-century interpretation of the formal French garden.

Bust of Aesculapius in the lime-tree quincunx.

The Queen's dairy N

Entrance to the dairy enclosure.

The dairy was built by Jacques Jean Thévenin from 1786 to 1787. The entrance is flanked by two round pavilions with brickwork window surrounds and piers. Their volumes suggest the silhouette of a dovecote.

The side pavilions

The pavilion to the left contains rooms for resting, whilst the one to the right, with its adjoining buildings, was used for preparing milk. In the coffered ceiling of the rotunda, four panels executed by Piat Joseph Sauvage using the grisaille technique are particularly remarkable. Sauvage (1744-1818) was born in Tournai and was known as a painter of flowers and still life compositions, especially on porcelain and enamel. He was particularly gifted in the realisation of *trompe-l'œils* imitating low-relief sculptures in bronze, marble or terracotta and often representing putti. His talents were widely recognised by contemporaries. In his *Essai sur la peinture, la sculpture et l'architecture*, the art critic Louis Petit de Bachaumont qualified Sauvage as 'an enchanter, bringing animation to his still-life creations and giving a sense of depth even on the flattest of surfaces; the relief is so well imitated that the spectator feels obliged to touch the work.' When d'Angiviller commissioned this work, Sauvage was at the height of his career. During this period he also produced *trompe-l'œils* for Fontainebleau and Compiègne. The theme dealt with at Rambouillet is the familiar 18th-century one of the four seasons, illustrated with playful putti: dances and flowers for the spring, the harvest for the summer, wine-making during the autumn and a bonfire for warmth during the winter frosts.

The Four Seasons, grisailles by Sauvage.

The entrance rotunda. The floor here was originally in white marble, with a central circular basin. During the restoration work carried out by Famin, a new floor in polychrome marble was laid and a new round table installed in the centre. Also made of marble, its star pattern is of inlaid porphyry.

Detail of one of the ceiling rosettes with oak leaves and acorns.

The central pavilion

The central pavilion of the ornamental dairy takes the form of a temple, built of carefully cut sandstone. The pediment contains a marble medallion representing a cow suckling its calf, the original emblem for the dairy sculpted by Pierre Julien (1731-1804), a celebrated court sculptor. The first room, lit from above, forms a rotunda covered with a coffered ceiling with rosettes carved in oak leaves and acorns in a reference to the surrounding woodlands. The walls are lined with panelling in white, veined marble. Tables, also of marble and supported by wall consoles, line the circumference of the room. The Sèvres china tableware was laid out on these tables for serving milk.

Medallion decorating the pediment: a cow suckling its calf, by Julien.

Front elevation of the central pavilion.

The dairy china

Set of recipients from the dairy service: these goblets, cups and saucers in hard-paste porcelain were designed by Jean-Jacques Lagrenée, known as 'the Younger'. The pieces were painted in the Etruscan style by Fumez (Sèvres, Musée National de la Céramique).

One of the armchairs from the furniture ensemble designed for the dairy by Jacob (Versailles, Musée et Domaine national de Versailles et Trianon).

Although they are largely forgotten today, dairy services such as this one, designed for the delectation of aristocratic ladies, enjoyed a brief fashion between the end of the 18th century and the first years of the 19th. Several major manufacturers made such collections, amongst them the Wedgwood firm which designed a special service for the Duke of Orléans, or the Sèvres manufacture which produced the entire service for Rambouillet. The pieces were commissioned by Hubert Robert and designed by the painter Jean-Jacques Lagrenée. Various buckets, bowls, pans, basins, goblets and vessels were used for tasting milk. At Rambouillet, there were also large draining pails for making cream cheese. Painted in imitation wood and decorated with rams' heads, they were placed in niches around the rotunda. The style adopted for all these objects, both in terms of their forms and their decoration, was inspired by Greek and Etruscan antiquity. The themes chosen, obviously enough, were shepherds and shepherdesses, sheep (probably merino sheep) and cows. A few elements from the original service, dispersed at the Revolution, can still be seen at the Sèvres National

'Breast-bowl' in porcelain, 1788, by Jean-Jacques Lagrenée (Sèvres, Musée National de la Céramique).

The sculpted 'N's on the consoles on either side of the doors (effaced in 1814 to eliminate the traces of the Empire) are a reminder that the present-day appearance of the dairy is no longer that of the 18th century, but the state to which it was restored by Auguste Famin from 1807, under Napoleon. A slightly earlier drawing by the imperial architect Charles Percier suggests something of the interest this project aroused.

The coloured marble flooring and the star-pattern table inlaid with porphyry are at odds with the original colour scheme where the unified white of the flagging and the decoration were in harmony with milk. An ensemble of furniture in mahogany was specially made for the dairy by the celebrated Parisian cabinet-maker Georges Jacob, executing designs by Hubert Robert. A few items of this ensemble still survive at

In the cooling chamber, the sculpture by Julien, entitled *The Nymph Amaltheus and her Goat,* was only returned to Rambouillet in 1953.
After 1811 and the Napoleonic restoration campaign, the grotto was occupied by a sculpture by Nicolas Beauvallet entitled *Suzanne at her Bath.* The artificial rocks are similar to those designed by Hubert Robert for the baths of Apollo at Versailles and to others at Méréville (Essonne).

Ceramics Museum. Some of them are later pieces, however, in a version created for the Empress Marie-Louise after 1810. The most celebrated and original piece is the 'breast-bowl' in the form of a woman's breast serving as drinking vessel, supported on a tripod decorated with rams' heads.

Cross-section through the dairy, by the architect Percier, about 1805 (Berlin, Kunstbibliothek). This rendering does not in fact correspond precisely with the restoration as carried out by Famin.

Versailles and in the national furniture collections. The mahogany tables, armchairs, chairs and stools were described at the time as being 'of the Etruscan genre' and were inspired by recent discoveries of bronze furniture at Herculaneum. At the threshold to the second room, known as the 'cooling chamber', the visitor discovers a fairy-tale setting: at the far end of the oblong space there is a chaotic structure of rocks in the middle of which is set the fragile and gracious sculpture by Julien, *The Nymph Amaltheus and her Goat,* dating from 1787.
Today, the effect is still impressive, but the visitor has to imagine the cool, misty atmosphere of the place when water jets sprayed from either side of the grotto and water ran sonorously over the rocks.

A sculptural odyssey

The bas-reliefs by Julien: *Shearing Sheep*, one of five marble medallions. The lure of nature is mingled here with mythological reminiscences. The scenes show an idealised image of the shepherd's life with characters in classical dress.

Apollo Tending the Flock of Admetus, detail of the second marble frieze.

From 1785, the sculptor Pierre Julien was commissioned by Hubert Robert to design the sculpted decor of the dairy. In keeping with the place's destination, the scenes were to illustrate the theme of nature's generosity: livestock breeding and milk production. Four medallions were fixed to the walls of the circular vestibule and presented the different tasks of the shepherd: *Milking Cows*, *Churning Milk*, *Shearing Sheep* and *Giving Salt to Goats*. In the next room, two long friezes were inspired by themes borrowed from Arcadian mythology: *The Young Jupiter being fed by Amaltheus' Goat*, and *Apollo Tending the Flock of Admetus*. Another medallion, placed above the door separating the two rooms, showed *A Mother Breast-feeding her Child*. Today we have the good fortune to be able to admire Pierre Julien's masterpieces in the setting for which they were designed. But it is worth recounting the incredible adventure of this ensemble of sculptures. The only one never to have left its original situation is the medallion on the façade. From the Revolutionary period, Amaltheus and her Goat left the dairy, first of all for Versailles, then the Senate and then the Louvre, returning to Rambouillet and the original grotto only in 1953.

The peregrinations of the bas-reliefs are an even more astonishing tale of itinerant works of art. In 1803, at the request of Josephine, they were installed at Malmaison to decorate the dairy there, and later the theatre. In 1819 they were sold by Josephine's son Eugène de Beauharnais to the British banker Alexander Baring. They crossed the Channel and were installed in a stately home in Kent where, in 1947, they were acquired by Georges Wildenstein, founder of a dynasty of art dealers. The marble ensemble, weighing nine tonnes, left for the continent again, first to Paris then to Geneva, eventually coming to the Louvre, by dation, in 2003. The works were then returned to Rambouillet where, after almost two centuries of travels, they were reinstalled in their original, sumptuous setting.

The English garden and its buildings

The shell cottage

The first garden building is the cottage decorated with shells, built by Paindebeld from 1779. According to tradition, it was designed for the Princess of Lamballe, the Duke of Penthièvre's daughter-in-law and a close friend of Queen Marie-Antoinette. Since the restorations in Napoleon's times, it is situated on an island reached by two stone bridges. An engraving by Le Rouge shows that these bridges were originally of wooden construction and far more picturesque in appearance.

The two small closed windows on the rear elevation of the cottage are fake, not corresponding to the circular plan of the room inside.

Ox bone fixed in the mortar of the wall.

Ionic capital and frieze, detail of the shell decoration.

The cottage has a thatched roof. Its millstone façade is in random ashlar-work beneath wooden lintels. Oxen femurs are encrusted in the mortar, a detail that seems curious today but which was frequent in rural architecture from the 17th century. The bones served to take humidity out of the walls and were also useful hooks for climbing plants such as ivy or honeysuckle that originally covered the pavilion. The interior of the cottage is a complete surprise. The ground plan is square but the room inside is circular, and rusticity is abandoned for an image demonstrating just how refined the age of the Enlightenment could be. The decoration, encrusted in the mortar, is entirely comprised of sea-shells, delicately mingled with mother-of-pearl and pieces of glass and metal. The fluting of the pilasters is tinted with red brick dust. Pearly shells from Dieppe, shells from the Seine, mussels and sea-shells from the West Indies are fixed to the wall by tiny, almost invisible nails. They are put together to form Ionic capitals with oak-leaf garlands, vessels, medallions, cornices and urns. The fireplace, with a real hearth, is surmounted by a mirror in which the visitor's reflection is surrounded by the sparkle of mother-of-pearl. The illusion of being in a dream world was reinforced by the furniture specially designed for the room. Set on the star-shaped parquet, the rounded divans followed the curves of the walls; the chairs, the little pedestal tables and the fire-

Bull-rush stalks forming the decorative legs of one of the chairs.

The privy.

On either side of the fireplace, the niches are decorated with baskets full of shells and urns.

guard all seem to float on the sprays of rushes which form their legs. This exceptional ensemble of 18th-century furniture has been kept up to now in the Marble Room of the chateau. It should be reinstalled in the cottage or given another, more appropriate setting. Near the entry to the room, a hidden door leads into a little privy, decorated with wooden panelling painted with birds and flowers. Two miniature automatons emerged from the walls offering toiletry accessories for the ladies.

The Chinese kiosk, engraving by Georges Louis Le Rouge from *Jardins anglo-chinois à la mode*, a publication on fashionable Anglo-Chinese gardens (1776-1789). Nothing remains of this structure except the rockwork foundation, known as the Lovers' Grotto.

Passage beneath the rocks supporting the Chinese kiosk. The English river flows from here.

The Lovers' Grotto P

Not far from the cottage, following the river upstream, is the Lovers' Grotto, so called on account of two young lovers who died there in 1792, struck by lightening. When it was first built, this grotto formed the foundations of the Chinese kiosk, a folly that no picturesque garden could be without, like the carefully arranged piles of millstones with spring water. This rockwork structure was restored during the 19th century by a certain P. Letourneau who specialised in rustic and Rococo garden structures which remained fashionable until the beginning of the 20th century. This builder has left the name of his firm encrusted in the stone.

The Farm B

This farm was built from 1785 to 1786 by the architect Jacques Jean Thévenin. Located at the highest point in the park by a lake, it is representative of the emerging movement for the creation of model and experimental farms.
The buildings are arranged symmetrically around a central courtyard. Lying on the central axis that leads from the entrance, a circular dovecote is flanked by two enormous barns. The brickwork surrounds and quoins underline the architectural forms and correspond with those of the entry pavilions at the dairy, with which the farm forms a harmonious ensemble. The side buildings are for horses, a herd of Swiss cows, sheep from North Africa, angora goats and moufflons, or wild sheep. The farm has been restored today for the visiting public and to accommodate administrative staff.

The courtyard of the farm with a flock of merino sheep.

The Sheep Farm C

The sheep farm, built in 1805 on the orders of Napoleon, now the National Sheep Farm, has become a major centre for the study and breeding of merino sheep. In a reference to bucolic Antiquity, an extract from Virgil's second *Eclogue* is engraved on a marble plaque still visible at the entrance to the courtyard: *Curat oves oviumque magistros*, '[The school] takes care of its sheep and of their masters.' The farm was enlarged several times during the 20th century, most recently in 1977, and is today an exceptional living museum of merino sheep. To discover the history of merino sheep and how they are bred, in particular the prestigious race of Rambouillet merino sheep, the museum can be visited all the year round, but the best time to come is on one of the special occasions in the sheep year: at sheep-shearing time, for the sheepdog trials with demonstrations by shepherds, or for the festivities at lambing season. The National Sheep Farm is also home to one of France's major agricultural establishments, a training centre in agricultural zootechnics which is housed in new buildings situated below the farm. This centre was created in 1955 in order to group together several agricultural schools, variously specialised in sheep rearing, poultry farming and artificial insemination.

The entry portico of the sheep farm, built to commemorate the arrival of the merino sheep in 1786 (Bergerie nationale).

From the domain to the town

The chateau, first royal and then imperial, completely dominated the development of the town itself. A visit to the town is indispensable for a complementary perspective on the overall history of the place. During the 18th century, several private houses were built there, along with other buildings associated with the management of the domain, such as the Governor's residence and the bailiff's court, designed by the architect Jacques Jean Thévenin. Under the Empire, the last major undertaking associated with the domain was the Palace of the King of Rome, built by Famin and linking Rambouillet with the memory of Napoléon's son, Napoleon II, known as the 'Aiglon' or Eaglet.

From the Governor's residence to the Palace of the King of RomeE

The Palace of the King of Rome facing the garden. The Orchard Pavilion can be made out to the left.

Place du Roi-de-Rome

This Governor's residence was built from 1784 to 1787 by Jacques Jean Thévenin for the Count d'Angiviller, governor of the town. The residence was demolished during the Revolutionary period; all that remains are the outbuildings which today line the entrance to the courtyard. A garden known as 'The Orchard', attributed to Hubert Robert, opens in front of the residence to join up with the royal domain, separated from it by railings. Dating from the creation of this garden, the Orchard Pavilion was originally built in 1718 as a house for the Count of Toulouse's valet, then integrated into the overall design in 1780. The simplicity of its elevation gives no idea of the richness of its interior decoration. Ten oval medallions in stucco still adorn the panelling, showing playful putti symbolising War and Peace, the Four Seasons, Hunting, Fishing and the Navy. In 1806 when the site returned to the civil list, the Emperor commissioned Auguste Famin to built a new residence to accommodate the domain's guests. Work began in 1809 but in 1811, after the birth of Napoleon's long-awaited heir, the building's

The Orchard Pavilion.

destination was changed, becoming the Palace of the King of Rome. After the fall of the Empire, the building was abandoned and its central part demolished between 1836 and 1841. Only the two side wings and two bays of the central building survive to show the Tuscan style adopted by Famin, inspired by the architecture of Florentine palaces: the toothed quoins, the bossage♦ of the stone at the lower level, the hierarchical expression of the different floors, the projecting drip stones underlining the first-floor windows, the overhanging cornice with its modillions.♦ Between 1836 and 1841, the buildings witnessed their last major alteration with the construction of an edifice known as the Imperial Pavilion, built on the axis of the central part which had been demolished. Since 1989 the ensemble, which belongs to the town of Rambouillet, has been used as a cultural centre. In 1995 it was given statutory protection as a historic monument and, since 2001, the Goose Game Museum has been housed in one of the wings.

Medallion decorating the Orchard Pavilion; the putti figures wearing helmets represent war.

♦***Bossage:*** chamfered finish given to the blocks of stone masonry of a building.

♦***Modillions:*** series of brackets or blocks supporting a cornice.

The bailiff's court, today the town hall D

Place de la Libération

In 1787, on the site of the town's former grain halls, Jacques Jean Thévenin built a new bailiff's court and a prison, the latter now demolished. The buildings were linked by a staircase permitting the prisoners to reach the courtroom directly. Louis XVI let this building to the local authorities for a modest sum and later, by a decree signed on 24 March 1809, Napoleon donated it to the town. The construction of a new courthouse in 1896 freed the building of its judicial functions and the courtroom was transformed into the council chamber for the municipality. The building was given statutory protection in 1965 for its architectural and historical interest. The central section has two levels, the ground floor faced in chamfered stone and the floor above, the *piano nobile*, finished in plaster with feigned brickwork. The façade is crowned by a Doric frieze with metopes and triglyphs. The centre of the building, in Saint-Leu stone, projects slightly and is crowned by a pediment. A sculpted bas-relief presents the figure of Justice with her emblematic attributes, the sword and the scales. There is also a putto holding the lictors' fasces, symbolising the authority of the Law.

Front elevation of the town hall.

Museums and Nature

Rambouillet can boast a rich architectural heritage, prestigious collections of furniture and a unique sheep farm. Alongside these attractions there are also some surprising museums and a vast expanse of countryside only a short distance from Paris.

A goose game, the *Grande Fête de Fouilly les Oies,* 1900 (Rambouillet, Goose Game Museum).

Museum of the Goose Game E

Palace of the King of Rome

This museum of the *Jeu de l'Oie*, or 'Goose Game', is unique in Europe. It was created in 2001 thanks to the donation of the Pierre Dietsch collection comprising some 2,500 goose games, a board game similar to snakes and ladders. According to legend, this game was invented by Greek soldiers during the siege of Troy. It re-emerged during the 16th century and is still a popular board game today, developing in keeping with the progress of new printing techniques. From the outset, the images on the board dealt with a broad variety of subjects: fashion, major monuments, religion, industry, costumes, gastronomy… The game can be seen as a mirror held up to society through the ages. Although designed for entertainment, it was used for educational or even propaganda purposes. There are games with the genealogy of the kings of France, political events, heraldry, natural science and general culture. Indeed, there is hardly a school lesson which the goose game overlooks, and recognised experts have sometimes contributed their knowledge. The oldest geographical game in the museum, the 'game of the world', was designed in 1659 by the geographer Pierre Duval. The collection is presented in chronological order, displaying a selection of the numerous boards of French and foreign origin. Their brightly-coloured decoration and thematic variety makes them a pleasure for young and old alike. For younger visitors, of course, dice are provided for real games. The last room presents a collection of games derived from the goose game or belonging to the same family: the monkey puzzle game, the steeple-chase game, the owl game. Temporary exhibitions renew the attraction of this splendid museum.

The Rambolitrain Museum E

4, place Jeanne-d'Arc

This museum was founded in 1984 by the collector Jacques Visbecq and the model-maker Alain Baldit. Its collection of no fewer than 4,000 model trains offers an overview, in miniature, of railway history through the ages. One of the aims of the museum is to preserve pieces that bear witness not only to railway history and the saga of the major railway companies but also to the development of the toy industry in general since the middle of the 19th century. But it is of course a place which delights youngsters and railway aficionados. Horse-drawn trains, steam trains and electric trains present the locomotives and rolling stock, along with metropolitan trains, trams and funicular railways, all set in landscapes with model stations, goods sheds, signals, signal boxes and miniature figures going about their railway business. The toys were first made by artisans, using wood or tin plate, but subsequently became authentic model reproductions of real trains, manufactured by prestigious firms in Germany, France, England and the United States. The objects presented in the museum date mainly from the years 1880 to 1960. The collection of model railway landscapes covers a later period (1930 to 1970) and comprises scenes from the major French companies prior to their nationalisation, the 'P.L.M.' (Paris-Lyon-Méditerranée) or the 'P.O.' (Paris-Orléans). The museum is full of movement and the magic appeal of the small scale. Outside too, the garden is full of animation. Loco-tractors and running miniature steam trains give the visitor a Gulliver-like sensation in a railway Lilliput.

A broad gauge Radiguet locomotive, 1885.

A Picasso rail-car on the $1/43^{e}$ scale network.

The 'Espace Rambouillet' H

Route de Clairefontaine

The Rambouillet forest, managed by the French forestry commission, covers 250 hectares and is a real garden of Eden. There are does, roebucks, wild boar, deer, stags and wild oxen living freely. When approached with caution, these animals can be observed at close quarters. A discovery trail, equipped with observation posts and information panels, helps the visitor identify the animals. In the middle of this natural space there is also an 'eagle forest', set aside for the preservation of birds of prey. From mid-March to mid-November demonstrations with birds in flight are organised by professional falconers. About thirty species of birds of prey inhabit this part of the forest: royal eagles, tawny eagles and booted eagles, barn-owls, tawny owls, eagle owls, falcons, buzzards, vultures... With their proud bearing, the subtle colours of their feathers and the precision and grace of their flight, these birds offer a valuable lesson in the respect of nature and its diversity.

American bald eagle.

Stages and does in the forest.

Short bibliography

Blécon, Jean
"Récentes découvertes d'archives permettant de lever l'ambiguïté concernant l'attribution des restaurations du château effectuées au milieu du XVIIIe siècle," *Bulletin monumental*, t. 152, n° 111, 1994, 366-367.

Blécon, Jean
Le Palais du Roi de Rome: Napoléon II à Rambouillet, Paris, Somogy, 2004.

Bottineau, Yves
"Le château de Rambouillet," *Monuments historiques de la France*, 1980, n° 112, 153-161.

Guth, Paul
"Un temple pour les réunions pastorales de Marie-Antoinette : la laiterie de Rambouillet ...," *Connaissance des arts*, n° 75, May 1958, 74-81.

Heitzmann, Annick
"Laiteries royales, laiteries impériales : Trianon et Rambouillet," *Histoire de l'art*, n° 11, 1990, 37-45.

Lorin, F.
Rambouillet, la ville, le château, ses hôtes, 1768-1906, Paris, 1907.

Waltisperger, Chantal
Unpublished dossier on the chateau of Rambouillet compiled for the Île-de-France regional Inventory service, 1983.

Captions

BHVP: Bibliothèque historique de la Ville de Paris.
BNF, Est. Phot.: Bibliothèque nationale de France, département des Estampes et de la Photographie.
CMN: Centre des monuments nationaux.

Front cover:
The façade of the chateau in front of the canal, seen from one of the landing stages, CMN/Philippe Berthé.

Back cover:
The Count of Toulouse (detail), copy by Jean-Baptiste Charpentier of a painting by Hyacinthe Rigaud, Office du tourisme de Rambouillet.
Front inner flap:
The Negress carried in a Hammock (detail of the 18th-century tapestry), CMN/Philippe Berthé.
Back inner flap:
The Palace of the King of Rome from the garden side, CMN/Philippe Berthé.

Visit
p. 30: *The Nymph Amaltheus and her Goat*, marble sculpture by Pierre Julien, CMN/David Bordes.

Chronology
from left to right and from top to bottom • Political events: François I, 17th century, Chateau of Bussy-Rabutin (CMN/Alain Lonchampt); Louis XIII, 19th century, Chateau of Bussy-Rabutin (CMN/Alain Lonchampt); Louis XIV, 18th century, Chateau of Bussy-Rabutin (CMN/Alain Lonchampt); Louis XVI, 19th century, Chateau of Bussy-Rabutin (CMN/Alain Lonchampt); Napoleon I, 1813, Column of the Grande Armée, Wimille (CMN/Bernard Acloque); Napoleon III, photograph by Thiébault, c. 1860 (Paris, Médiathèque de l'architecture et du patrimoine, Archives photographiques).
• The domain: see p. 3, 8, 50t, 53t, 27t, 29t, 29b, 56t.
• The gardens of Paris and of the Île-de-France region: enamelled terracotta frog from the workshops of Bernard Palissy near the Louvre (Jean-Jacques Hautefeuille); the flower beds at Vaux-le-Vicomte c. 1657, by Israël Silvestre, Paris, Musée du Louvre (RMN); Paris, Belleville park (Alix Sallé).

Photographic credits

AKG Paris: 1t, 11t, 19t, 21t, 26t, 28; AKG/Erich Lessing: 3b; Archives départementales des Yvelines: 9; Archives Nationales, Paris: 7, 26b; Bergerie nationale, Rambouillet/Ruoso: 25c, 25b, 59; BHVP: 27b; BNF: 2; BNF.Est.Phot.: 10, 17t, 21c, 24b, 25t; CMN/Philippe Berthé: 1b, 3t, 11b, 14, 27t, 29b, 31t, 31b, 33t, 33b, 34 to 43, 44t, 45, 46b, 47, 48t, 48c, 50t, 50b, 51t, 51b, 52b, 53, 57cr, 57bl, 58b, 60t; CMN/David Bordes: 1c, 18b, 30, 46t, 48b, 49, 55t, 57t, 57cl, 58t; CMN/Jean-Jacques Hautefeuille: 16b, 17b; CMN/René Jacques: 57br; CMN/Pascal Lemaître: 21b; CMN/Étienne Revault: 44b, 50c, 51c, 52t; Inventaire général, Île-de-France, ADAGP 2005: 4, 18t, 18c, 59b; Musée des Beaux-Arts, Tours: 13; Musée Crozatier, Clermont-Ferrand: 56; Musée de l'Île-de-France, Sceaux: 19b (Pascal Lemaître), 20; Office national des forêts: 63cb, 63b; RMN 15b (Gérard Blot), 22b, 54t, 54b (M. Beck-Coppola), 54c; Service Photo Élysée: 29t; The Bridgeman Art Library: 5t, 23t, 23b; Town of Rambouillet: 8, 15t, 60b, 61, 62, 63t, 63ct.

Collection director
Alix Sallé
Editorial coordinator
Frédéric Chaumont
Translator
Paul Smith
Copy editor
Barbara Shapiro Comte
Graphic design
Atalante/Paris
Layout
Sylvie Lelandais
Graphics
Marc Brugier
Production coordinator
Carine Merse
Photoengraving
Scann'Ouest/Saint-Aignan-de-Grand-Lieu
Printing
Néo-Typo/ Besançon, France

Dépôt légal: September 2005